blue california sky

poems by

B. L. Bruce

Finishing Line Press
Georgetown, Kentucky

blue
california
sky

Publisher: Leah Huete de Maines
Editor: Christen Kincaid
Cover Art: Sasha Jimenez French—*Everywhere Blue Sky*
Author Photo: Nathan Nazaroff
Cover Design: B. L. Bruce

Order online: www.finishinglinepress.com
also available on amazon.com

Author inquiries and mail orders:
Finishing Line Press
PO Box 1626
Georgetown, Kentucky 40324
USA

CONTENTS

YEARS GONE

Years gone, yet the memory lingers like mist above the mud-smell of the lakeshore, in any listless gray sky. After the spring rains, reservoir flooded, the waterline rose to swallow the trunk of the eucalyptus. We shimmied the great bodies of their limbs, leaped from their low branches into the silt-water.

Ashore, we smelled of mud. My mouth pressed to the hollow bowl beneath your sternum—that fragrance of marsh on your skin, the coming of my womanhood.

Mournful grebe-call echoes out over the water. For you, I'd have crossed deserts on my hands and knees.

IN THE BEGINNING

In the beginning, I consumed you, became you, slaked a hunger
I didn't know I had. Some mean animal in me was subdued.

I fall more in love with our aging bodies, our surrender to vanity.

The evening light here dazzles against the wall. These days, it
is enough just to have your name to call out into the darkness.

WHEN WE CAME TO LIVE IN THE LITTLE YELLOW HOUSE

When we came to live in the little yellow house in the countryside, what I didn't expect was the silence. Such nothing as to hear the water trickling through the kitchen pipes, my clamoring thoughts. And yet, I welcome the sharp edge it gives my days. The *keer-keer*ing of the hawk-pair echoes above the pines. They return to one another evening after evening. The dog whimpers. We listen for the sound of your car in the drive, of your heavy footfall on the hardwood.

WHAT HAPPENS WHEN THE MAGIC DISSIPATES

What happens when the magic dissipates? Some sleight of hand exposed, all dazzle gone. Love is more than just penetrating a body. And yet, I hold your name in my mouth. The way you taste: fuyu in late autumn. In every room, your smell. I enter you.

THIS IS A LANGUAGE

This is a language that chose me, not I it. And with it I can tell you, *Here is something beautiful*: the jay shakes the dawn from the blue of its body; the bright spine of the ridge at first light; the clefts of the peaches deepening. On the wind, the sound of a lone coyote, keening, calling the pack home.

ONCE EACH YEAR

Once each year, my mother cuts back the vines of the hops from the railing, replants seedlings, begins again. When my sister disappeared, my mother pruned the lavender in the same way, likely thinking of my sister's trimming stalks to dry in the vase by the window. This is what grief looks like, showing in the body, what we choose to do with the space around it.

In the days my sister was missing, the summer heat broke century—old records and mean flashes of lightning swept along the coastline, igniting forests of ancient redwoods. Everything was burning, as though all at once the world was ending. It was in my every dream.

The day we found my sister, lying in the ivy beside the train tracks beneath a blue California sky, we thought of how we'd narrowly missed being consumed, the photo albums in the trunk of the car, the flecks of black ash on my mother's white roses.

THERE'S ONLY SO MUCH I CAN DO

There's only so much I can do with my days in your absence. The dishes are neatly stacked in the cupboards, your laundry neatly folded and nested in the dresser. Twice this week I've mopped the hardwood floors, such a sheen they reflect the moonlight.

I over-thinned the limbs of the maple you like so much, clipped the branch holding the old hummingbird's nest by accident. I tended the winter roses ungloved, sucked at a bead of blood after a thorn pierced my skin. I tasted you.

Is this not a kind of love? The waiting?

THE SMELL OF LEMON BLOSSOM

The smell of lemon blossom is on the wind. Spring planting has started. The sweet peas have pushed through the soil. The squash starts its lean, begins crawling along the ground. Later in the season, we will take them into our bodies, becoming anchored to the land in some unexplainable way.

THE MORNING YOU LEFT

The morning you left the kitchen light was on. Some phantom sound led me to believe you were still here—making coffee in the small kitchen, bothering with the news.

I called out your name. Your side of the bed was cold.

SO MUCH WAS LOST IN THE HEAT WAVE

So much was lost in the heatwave. The dirt wouldn't take the water, as if already surrendering. The hydrangea blushed a deep brown—I expected this—but even the leaves of the aloe curled, the coneflower wilted into the dust. And now that unmistakable smell of death is on the evening breeze. The vultures circle.

ROSES ON THE STATE PARK OVERPASS

Roses on the state park overpass above a discolored stain on the highway below—northbound, fast lane. The week before a woman from the next town over jumped headfirst off the crossing into oncoming traffic. As we merge onto the highway, you see the scattered white roses, petals beginning to wilt, and remark on the selfishness. I remember my darkest years, the cruel taunts, dingy restroom stalls. And later, fists flying, a gunshot in the dark; a razor between my fingers, blood on the floor. Then, there, those roses: white as hospital sheets. I wondered if the woman chose to fall faceup, hoping for one last glimpse of blue sky.

ON CRYSTAL PEAK

On Crystal Peak—snow. A storm front moves in from the east over Watsonville. There is snow-cover across the valley on Mt. Tamalpais. The radio towers blink red, each flash a thud in my center. Frigid wind. Silence.

NIGHTFALL

Nightfall. The swallows retreat to the barn. They say sadness is held in the hips, anger in the mouth. These are the places I hold you: the pit of my belly, my throat. And the slow dances of the years, where do we hold them? In scars that mark the chapters of our lives, our told stories? The bats come out in droves. I feel the knock in my sternum, know this is the delicate cage that holds my heart.

NAME ALL THE WAYS A BODY CHANGES

Name all the ways a body changes. Ash-colored hair begins to appear at the nape and temple. We mark it, poison it; it slowly learns not to listen. There is a certain economy with time. Yet, still, we are astral bodies—it stays in our very marrow.

I can't remember where my grandmother was born. I can't become feverish as I am in dream. It seems most of the doors to my body closed long ago. There are so many unmentioned things we bury behind them.

A milk-white egg comes from every female body but will eventually stop. The dog is dying, her busied body slowing. For three days I drink the cool water from a High Sierra stream, expecting it to join my blood.

Evening presses down over the mountains. If I sit here long enough, the birds draw nearer. The stream will call my name. The trees will lean in as if to tell me something.

IT'S A WARM EVENING BEFORE APRIL

It's a warm evening before April and I'm planting wildflowers at the base of the peach tree: zinnia, cosmos, aster. I think of my mother, slender hands moving through the earth. This is why she never paints her nails. Earlier, we walked through the narrow rows of the nursery. Every so often she'd reach out to touch the soft leaf of a plant, recite its name. *Salvia leucantha. Mexican sage brush. Hot lips.* Now, I think of how, in a few months, bright colors will appear here from the soil. And again, I will think of her.

IT TAKES A WOMAN'S NAKED BODY

It takes a woman's naked body to halt the violent protests erupting in the streets. Can you imagine? The eyeing of the gun muzzles, the pluck of cold at her nipples. The level of vulnerability in the middle of that intersection. Or was it the way she sat and splayed her legs over the asphalt, caught the attention of the uniformed men, that brought the world to a standstill?

IT SEEMS ONLY A MATTER OF DAYS

It seems only a matter of days before the trees begin to leaf—
which is to say that spring has announced its arrival. The heat
brings out the snakes. The crow-dance over the oaks is slow.

I pluck an overripe orange from a tree at the edge of the
abandoned orchard, peel it absent mindedly. A jackrabbit is
startled and bounds away, the pale backsides of its ears catching
the light until disappearing into the thicket.

I bring an orange home in my pocket, later place it in the bowl
beside the browning bananas, remember the rabbit—bob of
white tail through the grass—the smell of citrus.

IN THE WIND

In the wind, a petal from the blossoming plum has settled on your lapel. I leave it be, liking how it places us here, in the garden. Somehow, tending to the gophers' tunneling brings us together after a bitter fight. A buff-breasted hawk comes to rest on the fence, and we both turn to watch it fly off again into the trees. You pluck a yellowed leaf from the climbing rose, stab the shovel into the dirt at your feet, and stand straighter.

Still there are patches of ground where nothing will grow. I plant and replant the same barren mounds. I can't help but feel like whole years of my life are missing.

Again, I claw another hole, this time for geranium cuttings, already thinking of its going brittle. Then from the corner of my eye, a small victory: dark green spears of Spanish bluebells are edging up through the soil.

I WOKE TO A GULL SCREAMING

I woke to a gull screaming somewhere far off, the sound making me think for a short moment I was somewhere else.

My fortune neatly folded into a Chinese cookie: "You will walk on the soils of many countries."

I SPEND THE MORNING DEADHEADING

I spend the morning deadheading the polka roses, planting new spears of aeoniums, then pausing to admire new color the warmer days bring to the garden: golden daffodils, red salvia, paperwhite narcissus. Air is thick with blossom-scent.

Such a brief time the plum tree is in bloom, quickly replaced by nascent, unfurling leaves. Petals fall from the finch's work among the branches. I rake them into neat piles until my back begins to ache, think of how later in the summer I'll gather the small bulbs of fruit from the same tree and make jam for the winter.

I SAW THE WAY GRIEF ENTERED YOUR BODY

I saw the way grief entered your body—all at once and consuming—and stayed, eating you away. I prayed it wouldn't bury you.

Beneath a pale day moon, the veil of the darkest night slowly lifts. The duckweed will soon grow thick over the small pond and choke its banks. The overwintered white daffodils will reluctantly emerge.

And in each white face, we will find her again.

I FIND IT CURIOUS

I find it curious what we remember about our traumas. Blue tile the color of a robin's egg. White sofa with blue stripes. Blue braided wool rug. Blue glass. Agapanthus. Everything blue. The sky was so blue that day, and reflected in your eyes.

I FEEL SORRY FOR YOU

I feel sorry for you. The irrational fear of the dark. That the one you love most doesn't love you in quite the same way. That you cannot harden, your batter-soft center caves in, absorbs every blow.

And yet, the moon smiles down at you. You are healing. The birds sing you awake to climb the mountain and breathe the crisp air.

EACH MORNING FOR NINE DAYS

Each morning for nine days I rose before the sun, made the long journey up the mountain.

Had I not been searching for it I wouldn't have noticed the faint blur above the horizon. The comet was only a wisp of soft light.

But the awe of it: its silent careening through the black of the sky as it makes its neat pass. I'll be gone long before it returns. Will my children see it? My children's children?

Will they, too, know how it feels to be infinitesimally small?

DURING THE WORST OF IT

During the worst of it, a woman lights herself on fire in the center square. A young boy goes missing at sea, the days of searching futile. The wind shook free the highest branches of the redwood and left the road impassible for days. The starlings preened their shining feathers, as if going somewhere. In those days, my entire life became that amber light of winter—the final moments everything is vaguely illuminated before dusk. My grief spilled over. No more can be said.

COME SPRING

Come spring, the poplars bud. The black and white cat teaches me patience, day by day draws nearer, less skittish. But when the young boy died, the cat didn't come home.

Every now and again, the white cross on the hilltop catches the afternoon light. I see this from my window.

The tulips keep pushing through the topsoil. At sundown, the pair of great horned owls call to one another from the thick of the firs.

A COLD MORNING IN FEBRUARY

A cold morning in February a bulldozer fell the tall, barren pine at the edge of the meadow. For years—perhaps even generations, at least long before I arrived here—the tree gave roost to the pair of red-shouldered hawks.

One came to depend on them, like seasons, the way of things. There was a kind of comfort in their perching among the bare branches, broad-winged sentry over the low field.

In the days that followed, the hawks keened, then disappeared, having been pushed from all they had. When the saws ceased, the piles of pulp that had once been the old pine neatly piled, what was left was silence.

Still my eyes wander to the treeline where the sun-worn branches rose, expecting the still silhouettes against the sky, their careful vigil.

A FEW DAYS AGO

A few days ago, it snowed; thick flakes fell slowly from the white sky. I watched the loft of them from the kitchen window, their thin dusting on the walkway, the leaves of the bay laurel.

Only for a few fragile minutes it stayed, a short liminal moment when it covered everything, then nothing.

I noticed today that the highest peaks of the eastern mountain are still snow-capped. In this I found a sense of longing—for all the things that never last, for something permanent.

LOOK AT THE PLUM TREE BLOOMING

Look at the plum tree blooming, the sour orange all but dormant. Soft buds opening as if to say, *Hello, I am here.* Somewhere downcanyon the wild hens are clucking. The quick-flighted bluebirds return in pairs. Shy, tawny kits surface from the den for the first time to meet the blue of the sky. The change, like the flipping of all the emerald blades of the iris in wind. The delicate light. Soft loam. I am here.

ACKNOWLEDGMENTS

Special thanks to the editors of the following publications in which some of these poems first appeared:

- "The scent of lemon blossom"—*Humana Obscura*
- "It's a warm evening before April"—*Red Wolf Journal*
- "Once each year"—*The Lakeshore Review,* (Nominated for 2022 Pushcart Prize and First Place winner in the 2023 Los Gatos Poetry Contest)
- "I find it curious"—*Bivouac Magazine*
- "It seems only a matter of days"—*Fulminare Review*
- "So much was lost in the heatwave" and "I saw the way grief entered your body"—*Riverstone Literary Journal*
- "Years gone"—*Blue Heron Review,* "Sanctuaries and Places of Peace"
- "This is a language" and "Nightfall"—*The Sunlight Press*
- "I feel sorry for you," "What happens when the magic dissipates," and "In the beginning"—*MOONLOVE press*
- "When we came to live in the little yellow house" and "In the wind"—*Gone Lawn*
- "Roses on the state park overpass," "During the worst of it," and "It takes a woman's naked body"—*Fevers of the Mind*
- "Name all the ways a body changes"—*The Winged Moon*
- "On Crystal Peak," "The morning you left," and "There's only so much I can do"—*Beaver Magazine*
- "A few days ago" and "Come spring"—*The Passionfruit Review*

B. L. Bruce holds a Bachelor of Arts degree in post-modern literature and creative writing from the University of California at Santa Cruz with post-graduate work at UC Berkeley.

An award-winning author, Bruce's work has appeared in dozens of anthologies, magazines, and literary publications, including *The Sun Magazine, The Avocet Review, Northwind Magazine, The Soundings Review, The Monterey Poetry Review, Fulminare Review,* and *Blue Heron Review,* and is a widely published haikuist with work in the *American Haiku Society's Frogpond Journal, Modern Haiku, seashores, Akitsu Quarterly, folk ku,* and many others.

Bruce was named Featured Poet of Homebound Publications' 2013 holiday issue of *The Wayfarer* followed by the inclusion of seven of her poems in the *Poems from Conflicted Hearts* anthology alongside Poet Laureate Alice Shapiro. In addition to receiving the Ina Coolbrith Memorial Poetry Prize, Bruce was also the recipient of *PushPen Press's* Pendant Prize for Poetry for her haiku series published in *THREE* with Poet Laureate Erica Goss. In 2023, she was the winner of the Los Gatos Poetry Contest for her piece "Once each year," awarded by Poet Laureate Jen Siriganian.

A two-time Pushcart Prize nominee and three-time award-winning author, Bruce's debut collection, *The Weight of Snow: New & Selected Poems,* published in 2014 by Black Swift Press, earned her the nickname "the heiress of Mary Oliver." Her second book, *28 Days of Solitude* (Back Swift Press, 2015) was written entirely during her four-week residency in the remote forests of Northern California. Also written during this stay, her

31

chapbook, *The Starling's Song*, published in 2016, was selected as the Honorable Mention of the 2017 Pacific Rim Book Festival in the poetry category. Her fourth book, *Measures*, was released in February of 2021.

In 2020, she founded and is editor-in-chief of *Humana Obscura*, an online and print literary magazine publishing poetry, prose, and artwork with a nature/environment theme.

Blue California Sky is her fifth book. Connect with her on Instagram *@b_l_bruce* and on Twitter *@the_poesis*.

www.ingramcontent.com/pod-product-compliance
Lightning Source LLC
Chambersburg PA
CBHW022051080426
42734CB00009B/1294